SCIENCE FACT OR SCIENCE FICTION?

CRYPTOZOOLOGY

COULD UNEXPLAINED CREATURES BE REAL?

MEGAN BORGERT-SPANIOL

Checkerboard
Library

An Imprint of Abdo Publishing
abdopublishing.com

Published by Abdo Publishing, a division of ABDO, PO Box 398166, Minneapolis, Minnesota 55439.
Copyright © 2019 by Abdo Consulting Group, Inc. International copyrights reserved in all countries.
No part of this book may be reproduced in any form without written permission from the publisher.
Checkerboard Library™ is a trademark and logo of Abdo Publishing.

Printed in the United States of America, North Mankato, Minnesota
052018
092018

THIS BOOK CONTAINS
RECYCLED MATERIALS

Design: Emily O'Malley, Mighty Media, Inc.
Production: Mighty Media, Inc.
Editor: Jessie Alkire
Cover Photographs: Shutterstock
Interior Photographs: Alamy, p. 5; AP Images, pp. 13, 15; Bob Doran/Flickr, p. 14, 29 (top);
Danny Lawson/PA Wire URN:26065647 (Press Association via AP Images), pp. 23, 28 (bottom left);
iStockphoto, pp. 7, 9, 27, 28 (bottom right); Michael Hicks/Flickr, pp. 20, 29 (bottom); Shutterstock,
pp. 10, 17, 19, 25, 28 (top)

Library of Congress Control Number: 2017961626

Publisher's Cataloging-in-Publication Data
Names: Borgert-Spaniol, Megan, author.
Title: Cryptozoology: Could unexplained creatures be real? / by Megan Borgert-Spaniol.
Other titles: Could unexplained creatures be real?
Description: Minneapolis, Minnesota : Abdo Publishing, 2019. | Series: Science fact or
    science fiction? | Includes online resources and index.
Identifiers: ISBN 9781532115394 (lib.bdg.) | ISBN 9781532156113 (ebook)
Subjects: LCSH: Cryptozoology--Juvenile literature. | Monsters--Juvenile literature. |
    Legends--Juvenile literature. | Answers to questions--Juvenile literature. | Science
    fiction in science education--Juvenile literature.
Classification: DDC 001.944--dc23

CONTENTS

CAUGHT ON CAMERA!

In October 1967, Roger Patterson and Bob Gimlin were deep in the forest of northern California. They had traveled there in search of the legendary creature called Bigfoot. The men had read reports of mysterious large footprints found in the area. They were hoping to see the tracks for themselves.

Patterson and Gimlin were riding on horseback near Bluff Creek when it happened. As they approached a fallen tree, their horses got **spooked**. Then the two men saw it! Less than 100 feet (30 m) away was a towering, gorilla-like creature. The beast was covered from head to toe in dark fur. Its upper back was hunched and its long arms swung as it walked.

Gimlin drew his rifle. Patterson grabbed his camera. As the figure walked, it glanced over its shoulder toward Patterson. Then it disappeared into the trees. But Patterson's camera had caught it all!

Patterson and Gimlin's video is strong evidence of Bigfoot. Researchers think it is unlikely of a man in a costume because the figure's legs and arms are not proportionate to a human's.

Patterson and Gimlin's story drew worldwide attention. **Skeptics** said the video was a hoax. But to many others, the footage was proof that Bigfoot exists!

Bigfoot is one of many mysterious creatures whose existence has not been proven. These creatures are known as cryptids. This term covers all kinds of unknown species. The study of cryptids is called cryptozoology.

Cryptids have been puzzling humans for centuries. Legends of cryptids exist all over the world. Some involve **bipedal** beasts, scaly serpents, and prehistoric dinosaurs. These creatures lurk in lakes, in forests, and on mountains.

Belief in cryptids is based largely on witness reports. Many people have claimed to encounter a cryptid. Some of these people have taken photos or videos to support their claims. Others have even presented hairs or other body parts thought to belong to a cryptid.

Cryptozoologists study evidence of cryptids. They try to find out if the creature is really part of an unknown species. They also determine whether the creature could be a known species or one thought to be extinct. Until a creature is scientifically identified, it remains a cryptid.

People continue to report cryptid sightings today. **Skeptics** believe sightings can't make up for a lack of scientific evidence. But unanswered questions have left many people uncertain. Could unexplained creatures be real?

Bigfoot sightings are particularly common in the Pacific Northwest, especially in Washington.

Humans have been **documenting** cryptids since ancient times. Early explorers heard tales of unfamiliar beasts during their travels. They wrote descriptions of these creatures based on what they heard. These descriptions were sometimes accepted as fact. And the stories of strange and **fantastic** creatures have been passed down through the ages.

In the year 77, Roman scholar Pliny the Elder published a collection of writings on natural history. One of the writings described humans with the heads of dogs. In the 1300s, Sir John Mandeville's collection of travel essays mentioned similar beasts. In the 1500s, popular books about the natural world featured detailed descriptions of unicorns, dragons, and **basilisks**.

Over time, some cryptids became widely accepted as creatures of myth. But many other cryptids have turned out to be real animals. Until the 1800s, rumors of an African jungle monster were thought to be myth.

The giant squid was described in books and by sailors. The legend of a sea monster called the Kraken was inspired by the giant squid.

But in 1847, the creature was identified as a gorilla. An Indonesian reptile species called the Komodo dragon was a rumored species until described by scientists in 1912. **Pythons** and giant squid are other known animals that may have inspired earlier myths.

Frank Smythe saw alleged cryptid footprints in the Himalayas in 1937. Investigations found the prints belonged to a bear.

Despite its long history, cryptozoology was not a well-known science until the 1900s. In 1955, Belgian-French zoologist Bernard Heuvelmans published *On the Track of Unknown Animals*. The book explored evidence of creatures that hadn't been proven to exist. It encouraged readers to keep their minds open to the possibility of discovering new and exciting species. The book was printed in several languages and was an international best seller!

In 1982, the International Society of Cryptozoology (ISC) formed in Washington, DC. Its purpose was to investigate and discuss cryptids around the world. It published a journal and newsletter discussing cryptids. The ISC ended in 1998 due to financial problems. However, a new organization called the International Cryptozoology Society (ICS) was formed in 2016.

Cryptozoology has remained a popular topic for people of all ages and professions. Today, people continue to search for evidence of **bipedal** beasts, underwater monsters, and other hidden creatures. New cryptids are spotted each year!

BIGFOOT!

The most widely known North American cryptid is the forest-dwelling beast called Bigfoot. This creature is also known as Sasquatch. It is believed to live in the northwestern United States and western Canada.

Bigfoot is known to walk upright on two feet like a human. However, Bigfoot is said to be much hairier and larger than a human. Witness reports have described the beast as up to 15 feet (4.5 m) tall!

Bigfoot has been spotted for hundreds of years. Long ago, Native Americans told stories of furry beasts like Bigfoot. Later, one of the earliest recorded Bigfoot sightings took place in 1811. British explorer David Thompson was traveling in Canada when he spotted strange footprints in snow. The prints were about 14 inches (35.5 cm) long and had only four toes!

Over the years, Bigfoot sightings have taken many forms. Witnesses have claimed to see dark, hairy figures walking among trees or crossing roads. Reports have

A cast was made from alleged Bigfoot footprints. The cast was more than two times the size of Roger Patterson's foot!

described glowing red eyes and strange odors. Others have described mysterious sounds. Hikers have reported finding footprints up to 24 inches (61 cm) long!

The Willow Creek-China Flat Museum in California features a Bigfoot collection that includes Bigfoot casts, images, and more.

Witnesses have also presented physical evidence of their cryptid encounters. Photos and videos have **depicted** footprints or blurry images of dark figures behind trees. Today, Patterson and Gimlin's 1967 Bigfoot footage is famous around the world. But the video is still widely debated.

Scientists and other professionals have studied the video for years. **Skeptics** say the creature in the video is just a human in a costume. But the case has yet to be **debunked**.

Names:
- Gimlin, Bob
- Patterson, Roger

Incident Date and Location:
- October 1967
- Six Rivers National Forest, California, near Bluff Creek

Claims:
- Sighting of large, gorilla-like figure covered in hair
- Sighting of footprints made by figure

Evidence:
- 60-second video footage of sighting
- Plaster casts of footprints made by figure

Status:
UNSOLVED

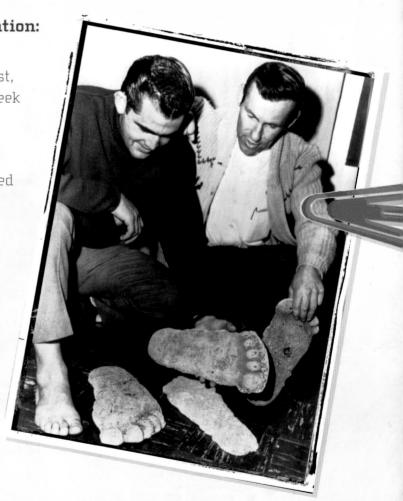

Thousands of miles from Bigfoot territory lives the legend of a similar **bipedal** cryptid. It is known as the Yeti, or Abominable Snowman. Like Bigfoot, the Yeti is described to be large, hairy, and bearlike. It is said to have gray or white fur and sharp teeth.

The Yeti reportedly lives thousands of feet high in Asia's Himalayan mountain range. It is difficult to climb the icy slopes of the Yeti's territory. Most sightings come from local people or experienced climbers.

In 1921, British explorer Charles Howard-Bury spotted large footprints while climbing Mount Everest. This Himalayan mountain is the tallest mountain in the world. Local **inhabitants** told Howard-Bury about the legendary monster that lived there. When Howard-Bury returned home, he told others about these stories. Word of the Yeti soon spread.

In the following decades, many Western mountaineers traveled to the Himalayas to find the mysterious creature.

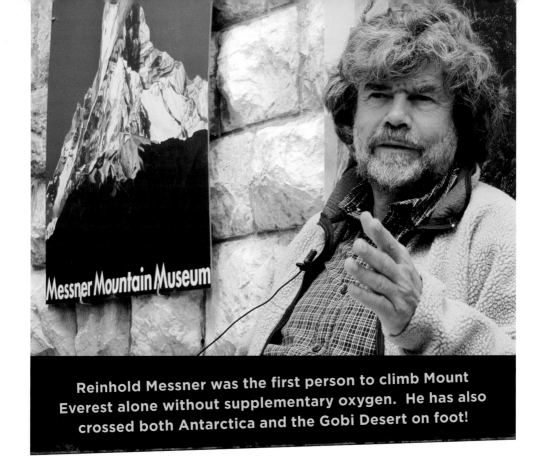

Reinhold Messner was the first person to climb Mount Everest alone without supplementary oxygen. He has also crossed both Antarctica and the Gobi Desert on foot!

One of the most famous Yeti-hunters is Italian climber Reinhold Messner. Messner claimed to have seen a Yeti during a 1986 climb. He spent the next decade searching for the creature.

Messner concluded that the Yeti is a species of bear. But the creature has yet to be identified. Travelers to the Himalayas continue looking for the legendary Yeti!

The Scottish Highlands are home to another world-famous cryptid. But this hidden creature does not dwell in forests or on mountains. It is said to **inhabit** the depths of Loch Ness, Scotland's largest lake.

The Loch Ness monster, or "Nessie," may date back hundreds of years. Ancient stone carvings in the region show a strange beast with flippers. The first written account of the creature is from the year 565. It tells the story of Saint Columba spotting the beast as it was about to attack a swimmer.

Sightings of the monster were rare until the 1930s. Then, a new road was built along the shore of Loch Ness. Travelers enjoyed clear views of the

FOR REAL?

In 1933, hunter Marmaduke Wetherell found large tracks along the shore of Loch Ness. He guessed they belonged to an animal about 20 feet (6 m) long. Scientists later determined the prints were made by a dried hippopotamus foot.

lake as they drove by it. But some glimpsed more than just dark waters.

In April 1933, a couple claimed to spot a large animal moving on the surface of the lake. Soon after, another couple reported seeing the creature cross the road toward the lake. Public interest grew as newspapers reported more sightings of the monster.

Loch Ness is 788 feet (240 m) deep and 23 miles (37 km) long!

People have installed sea monster figures in lakes around the world in honor of the Loch Ness monster. One called "Minne" was placed in several lakes in Minneapolis, Minnesota.

The Loch Ness monster has been compared to dragons, sea serpents, and prehistoric reptiles. But photographs of the monster show little detail. Many are dark or blurry. The most famous image of the creature was presented in 1934 by Robert Kenneth Wilson. It showed a dark head and neck breaking the surface of the water. Many thought the creature might be an ancient marine reptile. Others believed the photo was a hoax.

Official investigations of Loch Ness have also been inconclusive. In 1987, researchers used **sonar** equipment to do a deep scan of the lake. The scan picked up three large underwater objects. Scientists could not identify these objects. Further scans in 2003 didn't find any evidence of monsters in the lake.

Loch Ness remains a popular attraction today. The lake's supposed monster draws hundreds of thousands of tourists each year. Local businesses and boat tours encourage visitors to keep watch for the region's favorite cryptid.

Public enthusiasm for cryptozoology can make serious study of the subject difficult. Much of the evidence of cryptids is not **authentic**. Many people have constructed hoaxes to gain money, attention, and fame. For example, Wilson's famous Loch Ness monster photo was revealed to be a hoax in 1994. Such tricks have made photographic evidence of cryptids difficult to trust.

Sometimes evidence of cryptids is authentic. But after further study, such evidence is often linked to more practical explanations. For example, imprints made by stones or snow can look like unusual tracks. An animal's footprints can **overlap** and look like one large print. And odd bones and hairs have often been linked to known **wildlife**.

FOR REAL?

In 1881, witnesses in India's Madras Harbor swore they saw a gigantic sea serpent. Military forces attacked the supposed monster, which turned out to be a large chunk of seaweed!

Researchers thought they found monster remains at the bottom of Loch Ness. But the object turned out to be a film prop from the 1970s!

Experts also point out that humans are often fooled by their senses. From a distance, a tree stump or rock **outcrop** can look like a Bigfoot or Yeti. In dim light, shadows or waves on water can look like the Loch Ness monster. Such imagined sightings can be strongly influenced by belief in the legendary creatures.

Today, cryptozoology is a topic of interest among believers, skeptics, and even scientists. In 2014, a study was published in the *Proceedings of the Royal Society B* journal. It was a study unlike any before it.

The study **analyzed** hairs that were thought to belong to Yetis, Bigfoot, and other similar cryptids. It compared the DNA of the cryptid hairs to the DNA of known species. The study found no evidence that the hairs belonged to an unknown species. Later studies linked the hair DNA to brown bears.

Such studies represent a meeting point between science and myth. Cryptozoology is not recognized as a formal branch of science. But some experts argue the subject can still be approached scientifically. One of these experts is paleontologist Donald R. Prothero.

Prothero argues that geology and biology should be considered when exploring cryptids. For example, he asks how Nessie would have gotten into Loch Ness in the

Scientists think many Yeti samples come from the rarely seen Himalayan brown bear. Scientists know little about this brown bear species!

first place. He also points out that there couldn't be just one Nessie in Loch Ness. Other individuals of the species would also have to live in the lake.

Still, many people believe in the existence of cryptids, with or without scientific evidence. Bigfoot remains especially popular, with new sightings reported every year. Some people claim to have been **skeptics** before setting eyes on a Sasquatch.

Many people actively search for Bigfoot and other cryptids today. One is self-described paranormal investigator Jeffrey Gonzalez. Gonzalez has several images from Bigfoot sightings in California. He also has fingerprints and a cast of Bigfoot footprints. Gonzalez had the fingerprints tested. The tests concluded the fingerprints came from a gorilla!

There are also many television shows and movies involving Bigfoot. TV series such as *Finding Bigfoot* and *Mountain Monsters* **chronicle** real world cryptid investigations.

FOR REAL?

In 2012 and 2013, Animal Planet aired fake **documentaries** about the existence of mermaids. Afterward, the National Oceanic and Atmospheric Agency (NOAA) received many inquiries about mermaid discoveries. Viewers had believed the documentaries were real!

These shows inspire viewers to join the search and ask questions. Do these creatures of myth really exist? Whether guided by science or instinct, cryptozoologists keep looking for answers.

Many popular hiking spots in the United States have Bigfoot warning signs!

1847
A legendary African jungle monster is identified as a gorilla.

1934
Robert Kenneth Wilson submits what will become the most famous Loch Ness monster photo.

1955
Zoologist Bernard Heuvelmans publishes *On the Track of Unknown Animals*.

1967
Roger Patterson records what is now famous Bigfoot footage in California.

1982
The International Society of Cryptozoology forms in Washington, DC.

1986
Reinhold Messner claims to see a Yeti while mountain climbing in the Himalayas.

1987
Researchers use sonar equipment to do a deep scan of Loch Ness.

1994
Wilson's famous Loch Ness monster photo is revealed to be a hoax.

2014
Researchers publish a study analyzing hairs thought to belong to Bigfoot and similar cryptids.

YOU DECIDE!

Could unexplained creatures be real? You decide!

- Explore evidence for and against cryptids at the library and online.
- Research sightings tracked by the Bigfoot Field Researchers Organization and other cryptozoology groups.
- Read about the scientific method and how new species are identified.
- Head outdoors and do some exploring yourself!

GLOSSARY

analyze—to determine the meaning of something by breaking down its parts.

authentic—real.

basilisk—a legendary reptile whose stare is fatal.

bipedal—using only two legs for walking.

chronicle—to describe an event.

debunk—to prove wrong or false.

depict—to represent or describe the appearance of something.

document—to record in written or visual form.

documentary—a film that artistically presents facts, often about an event or a person.

fantastic—unbelievable.

inhabit—to live in or occupy a place. Something living in a place is an inhabitant.

outcrop—the part of a rock that is visible above the ground.

overlap—to lie partly on top of something.

python—a large nonvenomous constrictor snake found in Africa, Asia, and Australia.

skeptic—someone with an attitude of doubt or disbelief. Having this attitude is being skeptical.

sonar—a device that uses sound waves to detect the presence and location of objects underwater.

spooked—frightened.

wildlife—wild mammals, birds, and fish living in their natural habitat.

Booklinks
NONFICTION NETWORK
FREE! ONLINE NONFICTION RESOURCES

To learn more about cryptozoology, visit **abdobooklinks.com**. These links are routinely monitored and updated to provide the most current information available.